Ways to Play

WE PLAY SCHOOL!

By Kathleen Connors

Please visit our website, www.garethstevens.com. For a free color catalog of all our high-quality books, call toll free 1-800-542-2595 or fax 1-877-542-2596.

Cataloging-in-Publication Data

Names: Connors, Kathleen.
Title: We play school! / Kathleen Connors.
Description: New York : Gareth Stevens Publishing, 2019. | Series: Ways to play | Includes index.
Identifiers: ISBN 9781538231982 (pbk.) | ISBN 9781538228838 (library bound) | ISBN 9781538231999 (6pack)
Subjects: LCSH: School–Juvenile fiction. | Imagination–Juvenile fiction.
Classification: LCC PZ7.C66 We 2019 | DDC [E]–dc23

Published in 2019 by
Gareth Stevens Publishing
111 East 14th Street, Suite 349
New York, NY 10003

Editor: Kristen Nelson
Designer: Tanya Dellaccio

Photo credits: Cover, p. 1 Lane Oatey/Blue Jean Images/Getty Images; p. 5 Billion Photos/Shutterstock.com; p. 7 wavebreakmedia/Shutterstock.com; p. 9 Hero Images/Getty Images; p. 11 LightField Studios/Shutterstock.com; p. 13 mangpor2004/Shutterstock.com; p. 15 Alena Ozerova/Shutterstock.com; p. 17 Eternity in an Instant/Photolibrary/Getty Images; p. 19 Africa Studio/Shutterstock.com; p. 21 Hatchapong Palurtchaivong/Shutterstock.com; p. 23 Beatrice Mihaela/Shutterstock.com.

Printed in the United States of America

CPSIA compliance information: Batch #CW19GS: For further information contact Gareth Stevens, New York, New York at 1-800-542-2595.

Contents

Let's pretend to be in school.

Teachers help us learn at school.

Miranda pretends to
be the teacher.
She shows us numbers!

1 2 3
4 5 6
11 12 13 14
17 18 19
22 23

Jerome knows the answer.
He raises his hand.

Toby and Wylie
play school.
They like to
read together!

We paint a picture.
It is just like art class!

Ellen plays
the music teacher.
We sing a song.

It is time to practice writing!

Pete knows his letters well.

How do you like to play school?

Words to Know

numbers

teacher

Index